I0147243

STUFFED

Love Poems for Assholes

MAEGEN MCAULIFFE O'LEARY

THE FINISHED PROJECT
© 2025

All Rights Reserved

© Maegen McAuliffe O'Leary, The Finished Project LLC, 2025

No part of this publication may be reproduced, distributed, or transmitted in any form or by any means, without the prior written permission of the publisher and author, except in the case of brief quotations embodied in critical reviews and certain other noncommercial uses permitted by copyright law. Replicating, reproducing, remixing, and/or sampling copyrighted work without crediting the publisher and author is stealing. Violators are subject to prosecution under applicable copyright laws. Don't be an asshole.

ISBN 979-8-9918767-2-8 (print)
ISBN 979-8-9918767-3-5 (e-book)

THE FINISHED PROJECT

POETRY FOR REAL LIFE, IN REAL LIFE.

For Sean, because it takes an asshole to love an asshole.

CONTENTS

STUFFED

Wedding Day (4 July 2018)

THE FOUR HORSEMEN

The body is the instrument of possession.
The mind—prisoner of obsession.
The soul is the enemy of repression.
And the heart? Truth's confession.

COMMENCEMENT

Take off your cap
and touch me.

I am ready to begin.

THIS SUMMER

Swerve me
by the apple wood

tree. Keep spinning
and spinning the soil.

As with anything,
repetition is key

to success. Turn up
the history of things.

ON FIRST LOVE

You must feel desperate
longing once in your life.
Learn futility by chasing breath
outside your own lungs.

How deep
the inhale? A fast
from desire. How thick
the exhale? Blow

the whole load in one trip.
Fuck it. You gotta rip open
to lift off the ceiling. Learn to be
without and enjoy.

4

GOD'S RATIO

It's that 70/30
cold nipple

meets hot breath on pinned hips
unzipped by wet lips
spread wide for pushed tip.

How many springs left
in our bodies?
Count the balance

as I bloom. Run that mouth.
Take your talents to their natural

conclusion. There's no sense
in those buttons
left buttoned up.

I CAN SMOKE YOU

Under the table, you can drink
me under the stars.

Maybe we will
reach heaven alive. Maybe

we will burn up
on reentry.

TAKING THE CURE

My skin will not take the ink,
so I drink it straight.
I sip it neat.
I gulp it raw and hot.
It runs lifelines
down my throat,
carving canyons,
blotting out
this terrible thirst
for you.

SOMA

This body,
as distinct

from soul,
mind, and psyche,

it wants to rest
beside you.

It wants to feel
you breathe.

[A]BRIDGE

Isn't it beautiful to have someone?
Isn't it beautiful to have?
Isn't it beautiful?
Isn't it?

WEDDING SEASON

Oh   giddy   June,

    you   luckless

fool,   you   silly,

    hapless   babe.

POET'S PICKUP LINE

I am the best
        with enjambment. I break lines

to break hearts. The trick is to leave
        room for interpretation.

TINDER

Drunk with
you and
don't care

if we
get along
but we

get on
like a
house fire.

RELATIONSHIP GOALS

I want less of more
and more of less, but still enough

to stick it out. My love, that is the secret
to a legally binding, financially dependent, cohabitating

exchange of DNA. May this experiment prove
sound enough to outlast these weakly bodies.

May we love each other
to death. May you go first.

DISCRETE

Some mornings I think
who is this stranger

in the bed beside me?
The cadence of your snores

foreign. Your breath
a strange wind blowing

from a distant coast.
The tiny universe of you

spinning on its axis, silhouette
spiraling towards dawn.

DOMESTIC BLISS

Because truth takes the most courage of all,
I kiss my baby's cheek and say nothing,
which is not to say I am a saint,
or I have found enlightenment,

or the secret to keeping my shit together,
or the trick to not being triggered,
or that I've learned to identify my emotions,
or how to turn inward and embrace my wounded child,

or any of those excellent recommendations
from my therapist, who nods appropriately
when I tell him I am fine, just
a little overwhelmed right now.

It's just a phase, you know,
ha ha. It's just life, he he.
(insert shrug, closed-mouth smile)
No, none of that.

Because truth takes the most courage of all,
I kiss my baby's cheek and say nothing,
because twenty minutes prior I screamed
everything out into the void

where your face should be,
and I'm not positive, but I'm fairly certain,
the neighbors heard every word,
and I'm not positive, but I'm fairly certain,

(increase TV volume)
you did not.

LOVE IN THE TIME OF METASTATIC CREDIT CARD DEBT

check bank balance
transfer money
oh shit
forgot to pay the water bill   again
turn on auto-debit   overdraft fees
return to the office
unmask
remask
no mask
who cares   really
return to school
drop off
pick up
pack lunch
pay tuition
snot nose
rash mouth
COVID outbreak   again
breastfeed
co-sleep
couch sleep
fuck sleep
toddler's sick
baby's sick
you're sick
I'm sick
dog's dying
where's the schedule
what's for dinner
where are my pump parts
what should I wear
what's in my hair
I need a shower
did you go grocery shopping

did you get beer
did you stop at the pot shop
don't yell at me   I only asked a question
why do we feel so old
where's the lube
where's the condom
I hear the baby
don't cum in me   don't you want to try
for a boy   we did
he died
drink water
crush vitamins
go outside
go for a walk
fold laundry
clean playroom
make bed
empty dishwasher
scoop shit
feed baby
feed toddler
feed dying dog
sleep   when baby sleeps
I can't   remember myself
what did I   dream
fix resume
write cover letter
fill out application
submit poem
rejection   rejection
rejection   redirection
meet with HR   beg for my life
come back in 30 days
beg   again
keep going
stay present
stay open
stay soft

stay sane
regulate   my emotions
help baby
help toddler
help husband
regulate   their emotions
mom will you   play with me
mom will you   snuggle with me
mom will you   watch my show with me
mom will you   sit with me
mom will you   stay with me
mom
mom
mom
mom
mom   I love you
give baby to daddy   oh baby I can't
daddy can't   cope with crying
don't read the news
update LinkedIn
scour Indeed
scroll Instagram
God bless America
they shot everyone   again
water plants
eat vegetables
charge crystals
pull cards
count blessings
schedule vasectomy
I am doing my best   please
please   give me
give me   a fucking break

HAPPILY EVER AFTER

A scream is a wish
your heart makes.

Whatever you reach for
you break.

WHAT'S FOR DINNER?

What do you want
to know? No,

it will not end well.
It will consume you

like a wolf licking blood
from his paw—slow, meticulous,

indifferent to the howling
of hungry pups. You will become

pink spittle, a faint blush
clinging to his satisfied snout.

HOME ECONOMICS

My love, what a disaster
we've made of our lives.
Sloughing days down
mildewed shower drains.
The paycheck disintegrating
in the dog's bowl.

Dirty dishes stacked on
dirty laundry, piled on
dirty floors, crusted under
dirty bodies, laid
Babylonian beneath Amazon

boxes, beer
boxes, pizza
boxes, diaper
boxes, soda
boxes, weed

jars. Weeds
in the garden, weeds
in the grass, weeds
on the roof, weeds
by the road, weeds
in our hair, weeds

in our throats. This,
my darling, is the mess
love makes. This,
my dear, is poetry.

STATE OF THE UNION

I'm tired of the way you love
me in the light.
Turn dark. Wake beasts

from their slumber.
The moon makes strange
our revisions. We take turns

revealing each other.

YOU ARE INVITED

not to
      be. be-

come. come

      be with me.

IN THE HOTEL ROOM

We pretend
to be free.

I giggle and hit
your vape pen.

I don't mind the persistent suck
of the breast pump.

You say I get better
looking with age.

It is the perfect lie
because it sounds plausible.

There is no one pulling
and pulling me, just

your mouth.

SHOW ME YOUR STRETCH MARKS, I'LL SHOW YOU LOVE'S GROWTH CHART

pear ripened
fruit shaped
bowl bottomed
earthquake

thigh slickened
sweet cake
bare chested
sleep late

rum lipped
deep shake
knee quivered
soul ache

tongue shivered
heartscape
last call
death waits

PSYCHONEUROIMMUNOENDOCRINOLOGY

I cannot protect
what I love
without hurting another.

To be weapon and shield
requires both hands.
To hunt and to shelter

leaves me split between tasks.
That which I love
curls in the cleft,

makes a nest in the wound
and lies down to sleep.
The scar forms

canopy, blanket, and bed.
That which I love
dies pillowed in skin.

REVERSE PSYCHOLOGY

does
to make it
if you can't
mean to love it
if you can't
to take it
does

HEALTHY BOUNDARIES

Your sincerity breaks my heart—
so earnest are you in action, so naked is your need
to be received. I cannot help but love you less
for how desperately you love me.

DEFAULT MODE NETWORK

It isn't
the heart

or the guts
or the feet
or the groin
that does it.
It's the mind

that fucks it up
every time.

I HAVE NEVER BEEN HAPPY

except for now.
The tide sucks water
from its grave,
pulling teeth through sand
like love from split lips.

Gulls swoop
ribbons in the sky
and crabs dance
sidesaddle across
acres of seagrass
indifferent to their tune.

I am alone and strange.
I am right
where I am.
I have never been happy
except for now.

I HAVE NEVER KNOWN LOVE

I have never known love
that held me
that spoke gently
that said let go
I'll pull you up when you fall.

I have never known love
that freed me
that touched softly
that said run wild
I'll wait here when you fly.

I have never known love
that braced me
that warmed me
that said don't worry
I'll guard the door when you rest.

I have never known love
that filled me
that fed me
that said keep looking
I'll sing your name when you're lost.

I have only known love
that compromised
that strategized
that kept score
and picked teams.

I have only known love
that bartered
that traded
safety for sameness

and silence for solace.

I have only known love
that demanded
don't take that
don't be that
don't try that.

I have only known love
as losing myself.

BAGGAGE CLAIM

It is hard
to be less
of something
without more

to give.
That is why
we collect pain
instead of

letting loose
the past.
The weight
bears resemblance

to love's anchor.
It feels better than
holding open
empty hands.

ARITHMETIC

Two holes make
half a whole.

Two hearts cannot hold
wholeness in halves

if the hearts were not whole
before halving.

PALIMPSEST

I push hard against the pencil point,
hard enough to snap
the graphite tip into an avalanche.
My finger bleached with the effort

of push, pushing into the upward
curve of L, swooping down
to smoosh the blood out
over O, full stop—

I want this imprint to last.
I want the visible traces
to remain. The way I loved you.
The way I lost you.

Even when the surface is wiped
clean, it cannot be
written over, only read
another way.

RESOLUTION

Steps are often
the last warning
something is leaving

out the back.
Be the more fearless
version of love.

WRITE A POEM ON HOW YOU FEEL

Everything, in this heavy body,
nauseous with life. Write a poem
on how small you are, how
infinitesimally
insignificant you are to the cosmic order
that it makes no sense
to feel the way you do, little speck
of water and charge and calcium dust, exploding
with love and choking on sadness
because no one
held you when you didn't ask.

WHAT DOES MY BODY TELL ME

It wants? Three soft marshmallows
mashed in the cheek, a handful of cheese,
another, then another.
To rest, untouched

by God and men and children and work
emails dinging under the pillow.
The truth is I love
and I love and I love but am still

so deeply disappointed
by how ordinary this life is.
I try to sit in silent, sun-washed meditation
but the scratch to know more keeps itching

and I can't reach the treetop
where the crow caws my name.
What good is silence without peace?
So I keep loving and trying and sitting

and sucking corn syrup
through my teeth, and thank Satan
he doesn't want me
but you still do.

SHELTER IN PLACE

Love is not
the explosion.

It is the debris.
It is you and me

gathering splinters
for shelter, refugees

settling in the aftermath.

PENNED

There is never enough space
to feel what
I need to feel, but
a house is not a home

        without walls.

SELF : LOVE

It is snug here.
No one can touch

what only I hold.

WORKDAY

I want to wake
in the morning
before the light blooms

create life
before breakfast

then sleep
deliciously
in late afternoon

rise contemplative
for the evening meal

and at night
I want to love you

CIRCUMNAVIGATE

Tell me what miracles you know.
What shapes, what colors
form your landscape.
Let me trace
the topography of your tongue,
the shoreline of your heart,
the elevation of your blood flow.
Let me hear the drumbeat
pulsing at your temple door.

Tell me what miracles you know.
What stars, what saints
guide your dusty pilgrimage.
Let me scale
your ribbed plains,
your butterflied shoulders,
your tufted lobes.
Let me loose in your wild-
scented cedar grove.

Let me rush to find you.

BENEDICTION

Unburden yourself
    dear heart.

Life is only
    a spent dream.

AMUSE-BOUCHE

Everything is right
tonight, in our corner.
Babes sleep. We love

and keep loving.
We laugh
hard enough to choke.

SECOND HELPING

When he found me
in the pantry, suckling

my fingertips, my mouth
a chocolate halo,

and asked, what did I think
I was doing?

I offered only the obvious
answer—tasting happiness.

STUFFED

I don't know if it's possible
to have more than the sum
of this bliss. But if

so, I don't need it.
I am full up–
on love today.

ACKNOWLEDGEMENTS

Early versions of many of these poems appeared on TheFinishedProject.org and on social media accounts belonging to the author and The Finished Project.

"The Four Horsemen" and "Relationship Goals" were initially published in Taboo Tribune's *Dead of Fall – Issue 02* (2023).

"Domestic Bliss" was first published in Querencia Press's *Not Ghosts, But Spirits Volume 1* (2023).

The following poems were all previously published in *Bodies to Bury the Hunger* (Bottlecap Press, 2022): "Arithmetic"; "Circumnavigate"; "Discrete"; "I Have Never Been Happy"; "I Have Never Known Love"; "Palimpsest"; "Shelter in Place"; "Show Me Your Stretch Marks, I'll Show You Love's Growth Chart"; "Taking the Cure"; and "Workday".

"What Does My Body Tell Me" was previously published in *Full Belly: Poems* (The Finished Project, 2024).

ABOUT THE AUTHOR

Maegen McAuliffe O'Leary is a poet and mother from the Pacific Northwest. Her work focuses on the contemporary human experience as it intersects feminism, matrimony, motherhood, magic, creative expression, and the human body and its place in nature. She is the author of *Bodies to Bury the Hunger* (Bottlecap Press, 2022); *Full Belly: Poems* (The Finished Project, 2024); *Richest Bastard in the Poorhouse: Poems for the Proletariat* (The Finished Project, 2025); and *Stuffed: Love Poems for Assholes* (The Finished Project, 2025).

McAuliffe O'Leary is the founder of The Finished Project, a creative communications company inspired by the sacred feminine forces of creativity, courage, compassion, and communication. The Finished Project supports living artists and women-owned, small business through an online retail platform that promotes poetry for real life, in real life. Visit TheFinishedProject.org to learn more.

**POETRY FOR REAL
LIFE, IN REAL LIFE.**

www.ingramcontent.com/pod-product-compliance
Lightning Source LLC
Chambersburg PA
CBHW031806090426
42739CB00008B/1179